DISCOVERING THE UNITED STATES

Maine

BY DAVID J. CLARKE

Kids Core
An Imprint of Abdo Publishing
abdobooks.com

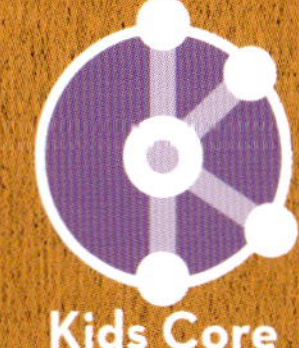

abdobooks.com

Published by Abdo Publishing, a division of ABDO, PO Box 398166, Minneapolis, Minnesota 55439.

Printed in China.
052024
092024

THIS BOOK CONTAINS RECYCLED MATERIALS

Cover Photo: Shutterstock Images
Interior Photos: Jesse Azarva/Shutterstock Images, 4–5; Shutterstock Images, 7 (top left), 8, 16, 25; Chris Dale/Shutterstock Images, 7 (top right); Nikolay Kurzenko/Shutterstock Images, 7 (bottom left); Marla Dawn Studio/Shutterstock Images, 7 (bottom right); Laura Zamfirescu/500px/Getty Images, 10; Robert F. Bukaty/AP Images, 12–13; Kingma Photos/Shutterstock Images, 15 (Life); Wikimedia Commons, 15 (Milton Bradley); Wang Ying/Xinhua News Agency/Getty Images, 18; Darryl Brooks/Shutterstock Images, 20–21; Tim Kornoelje/Shutterstock Images, 22; James Kirkikis/Shutterstock Images, 24, 28 (top left); Ben McCanna/Portland Press Herald/Getty Images, 26; Red Line Editorial, 28 (top right), 29; Sean Pavone/Shutterstock Images, 28 (bottom left); James Griffiths Photo/Shutterstock Images, 28 (bottom right)

Editor: Laura Stickney
Series Designer: Katharine Hale

Library of Congress Control Number: 2023949365

Publisher's Cataloging-in-Publication Data

Names: Clarke, David J., author.
Title: Maine / by David J. Clarke
Description: Minneapolis, Minnesota: Abdo Publishing, 2025 | Series: Discovering the United States | Includes online resources and index.
Identifiers: ISBN 9781098293895 (lib. bdg.) | ISBN 9798384913160 (ebook)
Subjects: LCSH: U.S. states--Juvenile literature. | Maine--History--Juvenile literature. | Northeastern States--Juvenile literature. | Physical geography--United States--Juvenile literature.
Classification: DDC 973--dc23

All population data taken from:
"Estimates of Population by Sex, Race, and Hispanic Origin: April 1, 2020 to July 1, 2022." *US Census Bureau, Population Division*, June 2023, census.gov.

CONTENTS

The summit of Mount Katahdin is called Baxter Peak. Hikers can follow different trails on the mountain, such as the Knife Edge Trail.

CHAPTER 1

The End of the Trail

It was August 5, 1948. Earl Shaffer had finally reached the top of Mount Katahdin in central Maine. Shaffer was at the end of a long journey. Four months earlier, he had started hiking the Appalachian Trail. His trek began in Georgia on April 4.

Shaffer hiked through 14 states. He walked more than 2,000 miles (3,200 km).

Shaffer hiked the entire trail from start to finish. This type of hike became known as a thru-hike. Shaffer was the first person to do this on the Appalachian Trail. His trek brought awareness to the trail. Each year, thousands of hikers try to make the same journey. They start or end their trips at Mount Katahdin.

Maine's Land

Maine is in the US region called the Northeast. Canada borders it to the north and east. To the south is the Atlantic Ocean. New Hampshire lies to the west. Maine is the only state in the country that borders only one other US state.

Maine Facts

DATE OF STATEHOOD
March 15, 1820

CAPITAL
Augusta

POPULATION
1,385,340

AREA
35,380 square miles
(91,634 sq km)

STATE BIRD

Black-capped chickadee

STATE TREE

White pine

STATE FLOWER

White pine cone and tassel

STATE CRUSTACEAN

Lobster

Each US state has a different population, size, and capital city. States also have state symbols.

Roughly 90 percent of Maine is covered by forests. This includes the central and northern parts of the state. The Appalachian Mountains run through western, central, and eastern Maine.

Maine's state flag features images of a farmer, sailor, and moose. It also includes the Latin phrase *Dirigo*, which means "I lead" or "I direct."

Beaches can be found along Maine's rocky coastline.

The state also has around 6,000 lakes. The largest is Moosehead Lake. Major rivers in

Maine include the Androscoggin, the Kennebec, the Penobscot, and the Saint John.

Maine is home to many different animals and plants. Moose, black bears, and Canada lynx are common in northern Maine. Tall white pine trees grow in the state's forests. Wild blueberries also grow throughout parts of the state.

Maine's Coastline

Maine's Atlantic coast stretches for 228 miles (367 km) if measured in a straight line. But it features hundreds of **inlets** and **bays**. There are also more than 3,000 islands. The state's jagged border measures 3,478 miles (5,597 km) when all these features are added up. This gives Maine a longer coastline than California.

In fall, Maine is known for the brightly colored leaves on its trees. Fall colors are usually at their peak in September and October.

Climate

Maine has four seasons. Winters are cold and snowy. Summers are mild but **humid**. In spring and fall, the weather is cool and often rainy. Hurricanes occasionally hit Maine in the fall.

Different areas in the state have different weather. Along the coastline, it is warmer than it is in northern Maine. During winter, northern Maine gets more snow than the coast.

Further Evidence

Look at the website below. Does it give any new evidence to support Chapter One?

Maine

abdocorelibrary.com/discovering-maine

The Passamaquoddy Nation has a long history of harvesting syrup from maple trees. Today, the Passamaquoddy have their own maple syrup business in western Maine.

The People of Maine

American Indians have lived in Maine for nearly 13,000 years. The state is home to the Mi'kmaq, Maliseet (Wəlastəkwewiyik), Passamaquoddy, and Penobscot nations. Most nations fished on the coast. In winter, they moved **inland** to hunt moose and deer.

In the 1500s, European settlers arrived in Maine. They came from France and England. They traded goods with American Indians. In the 1600s and 1700s, settlers and American Indians fought over Maine's land. American Indian nations grouped together to protect themselves. Eventually, settlers gained control of the land.

Over time, many European **immigrants** came to Maine. Since the 1990s, roughly 10,000 immigrants have moved to Maine from Somalia. This is a country in eastern Africa.

Some famous people come from Maine. Milton Bradley was born there in 1836. He invented many board games.

Today Maine's population is 92 percent white. It is 2 percent Black, 2 percent Hispanic or

Milton Bradley invented the Game of Life in 1860.

Latino, and 1 percent Asian. Less than 1 percent is American Indian. Maine's government recognizes four American Indian nations. These are the Passamaquoddy, Maliseet, Mi'kmaq, and Penobscot.

Maine is the country's top producer of wild blueberries. Some of these berries are harvested by hand.

Culture

Food is a key part of Maine's culture. Many restaurants serve seafood such as lobsters, oysters, and clams. Blueberries are also popular. Maine blueberries are lowbush berries. They are smaller and sweeter than other blueberries. Blueberry pie is Maine's official state dessert.

Famous Writers

Many famous writers have lived in Maine, including two children's authors. E. B. White wrote *Charlotte's Web* and *Stuart Little*. He lived in Brooklin, Maine. Writer Robert McCloskey also lived in the state. Two of his stories take place in Maine. They are *One Morning in Maine* and *Blueberries for Sal*.

Many lobstermen lower traps to the ocean floor to catch lobsters. Then they haul the traps back up. They throw lobsters that are too small or big back into the water.

Industry

Fishing and shipbuilding are big industries in Maine. There are more than 5,000 lobster boats in the state. Bath Iron Works in the city of Bath builds and repairs ships for the US Navy.

Lumber is another top industry. In northern Maine, there are many logging companies. Today, more than 20,000 people work in the state's lumber industry.

Dustin Delano's family has been lobstering in Maine for four generations. He said:

> Lobstering is not just a job, it is an amazing way of life. . . . It keeps our young people right here in Maine and contributes to our local and state economies. I am really proud to be part of a lobstering heritage that has supported this state for centuries.

Source: Melissa Waterman. "Lobster's Claw-Hold on Maine Is Strong." *Working Waterfront*, 6 July 2022, islandinstitute.org. Accessed 12 Sept. 2023.

What's the Big Idea?

What is this quote's main idea? Explain how the main idea is supported by details.

Portland is known for its historic waterfronts, which are home to many boats and piers.

Places in Maine

Maine's capital is Augusta. But the state's most populous city is Portland. Fewer than 70,000 people live there. Other important cities include Bangor and Bar Harbor. Most of Maine's population lives in small towns.

Acadia National Park includes more than 60 miles (97 km) of rocky coastline. Visitors can watch large waves crash against the cliffs.

Parks

Maine has one national park. Acadia National Park lies on the Atlantic coast. It includes 20 islands. One is Bar Island. It is a small piece of land connected to Bar Harbor. Visitors can walk to Bar Island at low **tide**. But once the tide comes in, the only way off the island is by boat.

Maine also has several national monument sites. Saint Croix Island National Historic Site features a French village from 1604. Near Mount Katahdin is the Katahdin Woods and Waters National Monument. Visitors flock there to see northern Maine's natural beauty.

There are many state parks in Maine too. At Camden Hills State Park, people can hike and camp. Popham Beach State Park is another popular site. Visitors can swim in the ocean and sunbathe on sandy beaches.

Vacationland

More than 15 million tourists visit Maine each year. The state is known as Vacationland. Most visitors come in the summer. Some stay for a short time. But others stay for weeks or months. Some small towns in Maine grow much larger during the summer months.

The Portland Head lighthouse tower is open to visitors only one day a year. But people can explore the grounds and visit a museum in the former lighthouse keeper's house.

At the Maine Maritime Museum, visitors can see many historic boats. One is the schooner *Mary E*, which was built in 1906.

Landmarks

In the coastal town of Cape Elizabeth, people can see the Portland Head Light. It is Maine's oldest lighthouse. It was built in 1791.

Bath is home to the Maine Maritime Museum. Visitors can learn about Maine's sailing history. The museum has a shipyard where people build wooden boats.

The giant troll sculptures at the Coastal Maine Botanical Gardens were created by Danish artist Thomas Dambo. Each troll is made of recycled wood.

At Maine's far eastern tip is a **point** called Quoddy Head. It is the easternmost part of the United States. The site is home to a state park, along with a historic lighthouse and a museum.

The Coastal Maine Botanical Gardens are in Boothbay. Visitors can learn about different plants and flowers. There are areas to learn about bees, moths, and butterflies. The gardens also feature five large troll statues.

Maine is a state full of natural beauty. It has rugged coastlines and scenic forests. It has many historical sites too. With everything Maine has to offer, it is no wonder so many people visit Vacationland every year.

Explore Online

Visit the website below. Does it give any new information about the Portland Head Light that wasn't in Chapter Three?

Portland Head Light

abdocorelibrary.com/discovering-maine

State Map

Portland Head Light

Augusta

Mount Katahdin

Maine: The Pine Tree State

Glossary

bays
small bodies of water connected to oceans or lakes

humid
describing air that has a lot of moisture

immigrants
people who move to a different country

inland
of or relating to land that is farther away from an ocean

inlets
narrow waterways that run between two pieces of land

lumber
logs used as building material

point
a narrow piece of land that sticks out into a body of water

tide
the rise and fall of an ocean's water levels

Online Resources

To learn more about Maine, visit our free resource websites below.

Visit **abdocorelibrary.com** or scan this QR code for free Common Core resources for teachers and students, including vetted activities, multimedia, and booklinks, for deeper subject comprehension.

Visit **abdobooklinks.com** or scan this QR code for free additional online weblinks for further learning. These links are routinely monitored and updated to provide the most current information available.

Learn More

Acadia National Park Activity Book. Little Bison, 2021.

Murray, Julie. *Maine.* Abdo, 2020.

The National Parks. DK, 2020.

Index

About the Author

David J. Clarke is a freelance writer. Originally from Helena, Montana, he now lives in Savannah, Georgia, with his golden retriever, Gus.